2014

FOOTBALL SUPERSTARS

BY K.C. KELLEY

SCHOLASTIC

Photo Editor: Cynthia Carris

cover left: Kevin C. Cox/Getty Images; cover top right: Jay Biggerstaff/TUSP/Getty Images; cover bottom right: Wesley Hitt/Getty Images; cover background: Danil Melekhin/iStockphoto; p4: Julio Cortez/AP Images; p5: Kevin C. Cox/Getty Images; p6: Andy Lyons/Getty Images; p7: Jay Biggerstaff/TUSP/Getty Images; p8: Jason Miller/Getty Images; p9: Peter G. Aiken/Getty Images; p10: Jim Rogash/Getty Images; p11: Bob Levey/Getty Images; p12 & 13: Michael Zagaris/San Francisco 49ers/Getty Images; p14: Steve Dykes/Getty Images; p15: Jonathan Ferrey/Getty Images; p16: Hector Acevedo/Zuma Press/Newscom; p17: Steve Nehf/The Denver Post/Getty Images; p18: Andrew Hancock /Sports Illustrated/Getty Images; p19: Zach Bolinger/Icon SMI/Newscom; p20: Hunter Martin/Philadelphia Eagles/Getty Images; p21: Drew Hallowell/Philadelphia Eagles/Getty Images; p22: Scott Cunningham/Getty Images; p23: Ronald C. Modra/Sports Imagery/Getty Images; p24: Jeff Gross/Getty Images; p25: Andy Lyons/Getty Images; p26: Rich Kane/Icon SMI/Corbis; p27: Rich Kane/Icon SMI/Newscom; p28: Larry French/Getty Images; p29: G Fiume/Getty Images; p30 top: Jeff Hanisch/USA Today Sports/Reuters; p30 bottom: Gregory Shamus/Getty Images; p31 top: Steven Senne/AP Images; p31 center: Rick Scuteri/AP Images; p31 bottom: Ric Tapia/AP Images.

ISBN 978-0-545-72219-3

12 11 10 9 8 7 6 5 4 3 2   14 15 16 17 18/0
                                                      40

Cover and interior design by Rocco Melillo

Printed in the U.S.A.
First printing, September 2014

CONTENTS

RUSSELL WILSON

QUARTERBACK

If you were putting together the perfect package for an NFL quarterback, you'd want a player with a strong arm. Check. You would want him to be mobile to avoid sacks. Check. You would need him to be smart to deal with all the plays and formations. Check. You would want him to be thoughtful and polite, to handle all the interviews. Check. You would want him to be 6'3" or more, to see over tall lineman. Um . . . would you accept 5'11"?

Russell Wilson knew he had everything it would take to be an NFL star. He had all the things on the list, but he had to prove that a "short" passer could succeed. He had already helped Wisconsin make it to the Rose Bowl and had shown his multitalented skills in three college seasons. But he was the sixth quarterback taken in the 2012 NFL Draft. That gave him fuel to succeed: He wanted to show the NFL that they should not have waited so long!

Wilson earned the starting spot in training camp and, almost overnight, the Seahawks were one of the league's top teams. Wilson was a steady hand, doing all the little things right—making the key pass, running for a first down (or even scoring), saying the right things to reporters. He let defensive star Richard Sherman do the talking and "Beast Mode" running back Marshawn Lynch hit the end zone. Wilson just kept winning. In fact, his 24 wins in his first two seasons are the most ever by a starting QB.

In 2013, Wilson kept his steady play going, leading the Seahawks to the NFC Champion-ship. In Super Bowl XLVIII, he really showed those other teams and those higher-drafted QBs. He threw two touchdown passes and was 18 for 25, flawlessly leading Seattle to a 43–8 win.

One more thing an NFL QB needs—a shiny Super Bowl ring. Check.

WILSON'S BIG DAY

December 16, 2012: Late in his rookie season, Wilson put all his weapons to work in a 50–17 blowout of the Bills. He rushed for a career-high three touchdowns while also throwing for another score. He also completed 71 percent of his passes.

▶ FACT FILE:

Rookie Season	2012
Years in League	2
Pass Attempts	800
Completions	509
Touchdowns	52
Passing Yards	6,475
Interceptions	19
Career Passer Rating	100.6

RUSSELL WILSON

Height:	Weight:	College:
5'-11"	203 lbs.	Wisconsin

* Drafted in 2011, third round by the Seattle Seahawks

▶ Led his Virginia high school team to state title.

▶ A baseball star, he was drafted by the Texas Rangers minor league team.

▶ 52 TD passes in first two NFL seasons tied for second-most all-time.

RUSSELL WILSON

JAMAAL CHARLES
RUNNING BACK

Football can be a tough sport. Injuries can knock any player out of the game. But the real stars fight back to return to the field and help their team. Jamaal Charles is one of those.

Charles joined the Chiefs as a third-round pick in 2008. He had starred at Texas, helping the Longhorns win a national title. Though he split time with Thomas Jones at first, by 2010, Charles was the featured back. His 1,467 rushing yards were second in the NFL. But then Charles went down with a knee injury. He missed the rest of 2011, but worked hard to get better. The hard work paid off with a huge 2012 season. Charles ran for a career-high 1,509 yards and returned to the Pro Bowl. But the Chiefs' 2-14 record that season gave him another reason to battle back.

Charles was a huge part of the Chiefs' amazing start to the 2013 season. They reeled off nine straight victories, and Charles scored eight times during that run. He ended up playing in 15 of the team's 16 games and led the team with 70 receptions. Charles also totaled 1,287 rushing yards, which led the AFC and was third in the NFL. Chiefs fans have watched some great running backs over the years—Mike Garrett, Christian Okoye, Priest Holmes, etc.—but only Charles has four 1,000-yard seasons in Kansas City. Best of all, Charles had 19 touchdowns, most of any player in the NFL at any position.

The Chiefs' season ended in disappointment with a stunning first-round playoff loss. But with the solid play of quarterback Alex Smith backing up Charles's game-breaking runs, Kansas City looks to do even better in 2014.

CHARLES'S BIG DAY

December 15, 2013: With five touchdowns, Charles set a Chiefs single-game record and was one short of tying the NFL record. He caught four TD passes and ripped off a 71-yard run for his fifth score. He was the first NFL player ever with four TD catches and a TD run.

▶ FACT FILE:

Rookie Season	2008
Years in League	6
Rushing Attempts	1,043
Rushing Touchdowns	29
Rushing Yards	5,823
Receiving Yards	1,975
Receiving Touchdowns	14

JAMAAL CHARLES

Height:	Weight:	College:
6'-1"	200 lbs.	University of Texas

* Drafted in 2008 — third round by the Kansas City Chiefs

▶ Charles was a freshman when Texas won the 2005 national championship.

▶ In 2010, his 80-yard TD run was the longest in the NFL.

▶ Charles has been named to three Pro Bowl teams.

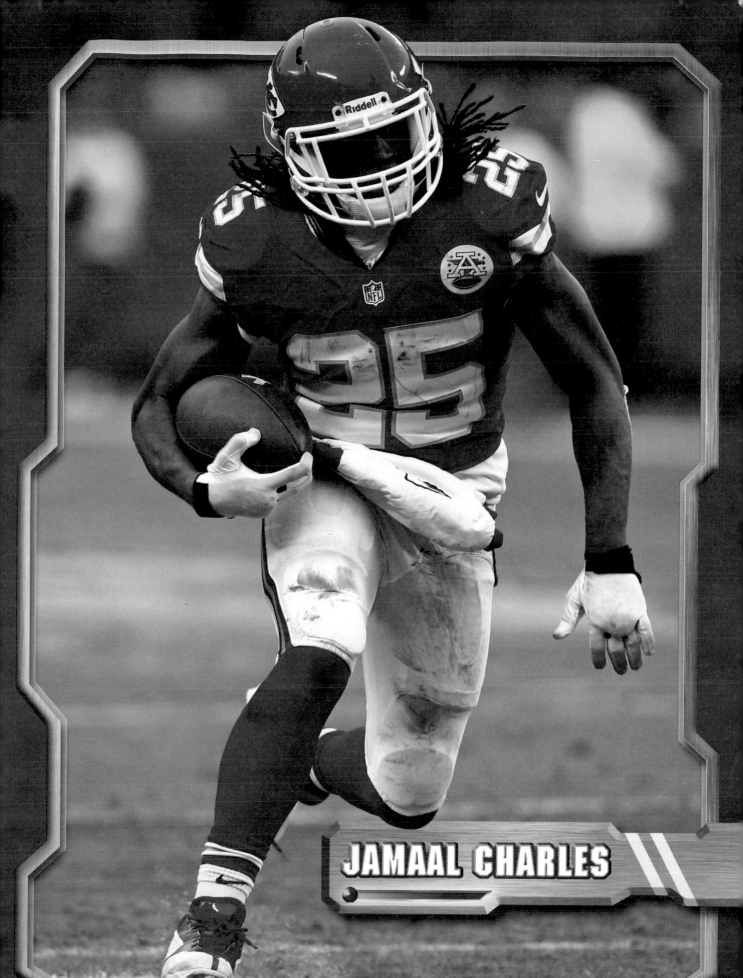

JAMAAL CHARLES

JOE THOMAS
TACKLE

Most NFL players end their season by emptying their lockers and heading home. But ever since Joe Thomas joined the Browns as a rookie in 2007, he has ended each season with one more game. This outstanding offensive tackle has been named to the Pro Bowl after every one of his seven NFL seasons. But success like that was almost expected after what Thomas did before he got to the Browns.

Thomas grew up in Wisconsin, where he was such a great athlete that he was all-state on both offensive and defensive lines for his high school team. He stayed local by going to the University of Wisconsin. Thomas was an All-America as a junior and a senior. He won the 2006 Outland Trophy, given to the top interior lineman—offense or defense—in the country.

Cleveland chose Thomas with the third overall pick in the 2007 draft and he's been a rock there ever since. He was so good in his first season that he finished second in Rookie of the Year voting—a rare feat for a lineman. His all-around skills established him as the best tackle in the league over the next half-dozen seasons.

Thomas is huge (6'-7", 311 pounds) but he's also very quick on his feet. This combination makes it almost impossible for pass-rushers to get around him. Imagine seeing that guy coming at you when he pulls downfield to block on running plays!

In 2014, Thomas will have another big challenge: Keeping Johnny Manziel, the Heisman-Trophy-winning quarterback, safe. Manziel was drafted by the Browns in the first round. If he sees action, the guy known as "Johnny Football" will depend on Thomas and the other O-linemen to give him time to work his magic.

THOMAS'S BIG DAY

December 20, 2009: Joe Thomas didn't touch the football in this game, but without him, it might not have been historic. Cleveland running back Jerome Harrison ran for 286 yards, the third-most in a game in NFL history. Leading the way on many of his runs was the man-mountain, Joe Thomas.

▶ **FACT FILE:**

Rookie Season	2007
Years in League	7

JOE THOMAS

Height:	Weight:	College:
6'-7"	311 lbs.	Wisconsin

* *Drafted in 2007 — first round by Cleveland Browns*

▶ *Thomas actually played tight end as a freshman at Wisconsin.*

▶ *Threw the shot put and discus for high school and college track teams.*

▶ *One of only 12 NFL players ever to reach Pro Bowls in first seven seasons.*

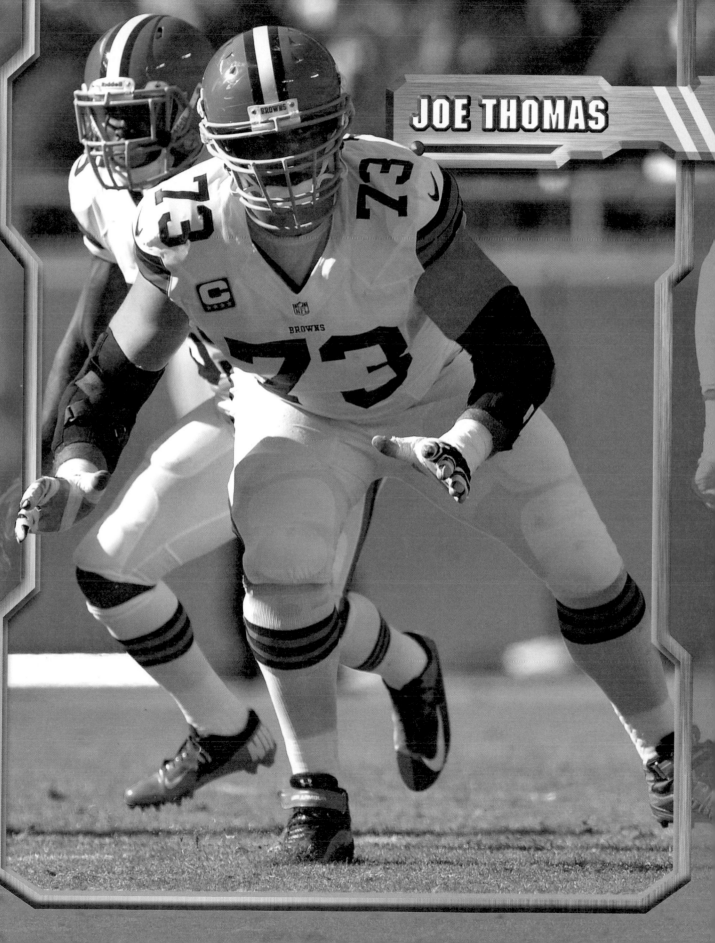

JOE THOMAS

STEPHEN GOSTKOWSKI

KICKER

The only way to win in the NFL is to score more points than the other team. And while running backs and quarterbacks get all the headlines, kickers get all the points. For the past seven years, a kicker has led the NFL in scoring. In 2013, the top 17 scorers were all kickers. And at the top of that heap of points was Stephen Gostkowski. His booming, accurate leg scored a league-leading (and career-best) 158 points for the Patriots.

Gostkowski took over the kicking duties in 2006 as a rookie, replacing Super Bowl hero Adam Vinatieri. By his second season, 2007, Gostkowski was taking advantage of a powerful Patriots offense. The team scored 74 touchdowns and their kicker was perfect on the extra-point attempt every time, leading the league in that department. The next year, however, New England needed more from Gostkowski. The offense sputtered, scoring only 40 TDs. Gostkowski made up for that by nailing 36 field goals, still the second-most of his career and enough to lead the league in 2008. That was also the first time he led the NFL in scoring.

Though he missed part of 2010 with an injury, he came back strong and has led the NFL in scoring the past two seasons. He has missed only one of his 400 career point-after attempts, while also making more than 85 percent of his field-goal tries. Add to that his explosive kickoffs that regularly leave the end zone and you've got the complete kicker . . . and a secret scorer!

GOSTKOWSKI'S BIG DAY

December 21, 2008: The Patriots romped over the Cardinals, and Gostkowski was a big reason. He nailed all five extra-point attempts, but he was also four-for-four on field goals for a career-high 19 points.

▶ FACT FILE:

Rookie Season	2006
Years in League	8
Points Scored	1,023
Field Goals	208
PATs	400
Longest Field Goal	54 yards (2013)

STEPHEN GOSTKOWSKI

Height:	Weight:	College:
6'-3"	200 lbs.	Memphis University

* Drafted in 2006 — fourth round by the New England Patriots

▶ In 2007, was a perfect 74-for-74 in PATs (Points After Touchdown).

▶ Led NFL in field goals in 2008 and 2013.

▶ Has scored at least 100 points in every one of his full NFL seasons.

STEPHEN GOSTKOWSKI

NAVORRO BOWMAN

LINEBACKER

How tough is NaVorro Bowman? In the 2013 NFC Championship Game, Bowman was seriously injured. In a goal-line scramble, he forced a fumble by Seattle's Jermaine Kearse. As he grabbed the ball, Bowman was hit in the knee. It bent back gruesomely, but he continued to dig for the ball, even as he was in obvious pain. Unfortunately, not only was he injured, Seattle kept the ball. The Seahawks ended up winning the game, too.

Giving his all for his team is nothing new for Bowman, who will miss at least half of the 2014 season recovering from the injury.

As a high school player in Maryland, he had to go through a similar injury rehab. In his junior season, he was the state defensive player of the year . . . and he also scored 22 touchdowns as a running back! But when he was a senior, he missed almost all his team's games with a shoulder injury. In college, he bounced back to have a fantastic career at Penn State. But once again, he faced adversity. He was suspended from the team for a while as a freshman for breaking team rules. In his sophomore year, two people close to him died right before big games. Once again, he came back and his All-American junior season led him to the NFL.

After a rookie season with the Niners as a backup, he became a full-time starter in 2012 and has never looked back. With him at outside linebacker, San Francisco has been to three straight NFC Championship Games. Tough, smart, and super-fast, NaVorro excels at shutting down the running game. When called on, he can attack the passer or even drop into coverage. His all-around athletic abilities make him one of the game's best at his position.

BOWMAN'S BIG DAY

December 23, 2013: NaVarro played a big part in the Niners' key win over the Falcons. He had nine solo tackles and a sack. He also returned an interception 89 yards for a touchdown, his first in the NFL.

▶ FACT FILE:

Rookie Season	2010
Years in League	4
Tackles	367
Sacks	9.0
Interceptions	3

NAVORRO BOWMAN

Height:	Weight:	College:
6'-1"	230 lbs.	Penn State

* Drafted in 2010 — third round by the San Francisco 49ers

▶ Set a Rose Bowl record with five tackles for loss in 2010 game.

▶ Named to the 2012 and 2013 Pro Bowls.

▶ Partly because of NaVorro's injury, in March 2014, the NFL passed a new rule that would let officials review similar fumble plays.

NAVORRO BOWMAN

MARSHAWN LYNCH
RUNNING BACK

As you could tell from Marshawn Lynch's attitude at Super Bowl XLVIII's Media Day, he'd rather do his talking on the field. Lynch was nearly silent during the run-up to the team's big 2013 NFL championship. But the man known as "Beast Mode" was not playing for reporters . . . he was playing for the ring. Lynch's power running was the offensive key to the Seahawks' first Super Bowl–winning season.

Lynch grew up in Oakland, where he was one of the top high school running backs in the state. He went to the nearby University of California at Berkeley. By the time he was a senior, he was the Pac-10 offensive player of the year and an All-America selection. Chosen by the Buffalo Bills with the 12th pick of the 2007 draft, he topped 1,000 yards in each of his first two seasons. But he saw his carries reduced in Buffalo until he was traded during the 2010 season to Seattle.

It was the best thing that ever happened to Lynch and the Seahawks.

Under new coach Pete Carroll, Seattle focused on the ground game, and Lynch was the right man for the job. He racked up 1,204 yards in 2011 and made his second Pro Bowl. In 2012, he did even better, with 1,590 yards, third in the NFL. In 2013, Lynch led the NFL with 12 rushing touchdowns, but more important, his power running drove Seattle to the NFC championship.

In Super Bowl XLVIII, Lynch only rushed for 39 yards. He did, however, score a key touchdown early in the game as Seattle was establishing a dominant pattern in their Super Bowl victory.

Seattle fans don't care whether Lynch gives snappy quotes to TV guys . . . as long as he keeps powering the football down the field.

LYNCH'S BIG DAY

December 9, 2012: In a game where several Seattle players had big days, Lynch was the biggest. He ran for 128 yards and scored a career-high three times, as the Seahawks romped over the Cardinals, 58–0.

▶ FACT FILE:

Rookie Season	2007
Years in League	7
Rushing Attempts	1,753
Rushing Touchdowns	58
Rushing Yards	7,389
Receiving Yards	1,532
Receiving Touchdowns	5

MARSHAWN LYNCH

Height:	Weight:	College:
5'-11"	215 lbs.	California

* Drafted in 2007, first round by the Buffalo Bills

▶ As a freshman at Cal, Lynch helped the Bears reach their highest ranking in decades.

▶ His uncle, Lorenzo Lynch, played in the NFL for 11 seasons.

▶ Got his "Beast Mode" nickname from the Transformers robot toys.

MARSHAWN LYNCH

PEYTON MANNING

QUARTERBACK

This whole page could easily be filled with numbers. In 16 Hall of Fame seasons in the NFL, Peyton Manning has put up enough amazing numbers to crash a calculator. But numbers only tell a small part of his story, one of the best and brightest in NFL history.

Following in the footsteps of his father, Archie, who was also an NFL QB, Manning was one of the best college passers ever at Tennessee. He was handed the starting job for the Indianapolis Colts as a rookie in 1998 and led the league in interceptions as the Colts won just three games.

Over the next decade, however, Manning helped turn the Colts around. They had only one more losing season until he left the team due to a neck injury in 2011. His passing skills played a big part, but it was his leadership and his drive that sealed the deal. A student of the game, he soon was calling many of the team's plays. He refused to let his teammates quit and he never let them down. For a superstar, he is also humble, rarely accepting praise and always praising his teammates.

Manning led the Colts to a Super Bowl win after the 2005 season, knocking off the Bears in Super Bowl XLI.

He was 35 when he hurt his neck and many thought he might not ever play again. But Manning showed that he was not just numbers, he was a player. Joining Denver after his neck healed in 2012, he turned around another team. He led the Broncos to back-to-back 13-win seasons and into a spot in Super Bowl XLVIII. And just to toss in a few of those numbers: The Broncos set a new NFL scoring record in 2013 with 606 points, while Manning set single-season records with 55 touchdown passes and 5,477 passing yards. Plus, Manning won his fifth NFL MVP award.

The only number left in Manning's career will be how many votes he gets for a spot in the Hall of Fame.

MANNING'S BIG DAY

September 5, 2013: There are a lot to choose from in his long career, so let's go with the most recent. Manning became only the fifth player ever to throw seven TD passes in one game. The Broncos kicked off a great season with a 49–27 win over the defending Super Bowl champion Ravens.

▶ FACT FILE:

Rookie Season	1998
Years in League	16
Pass Attempts	8,452
Completions	5,532
Touchdowns	491
Passing Yards	64,964
Interceptions	219
Career Passer Rating	97.2

PEYTON MANNING

Height:	Weight:	College:
6'-5"	230 lbs.	Tennessee

*Drafted in 1998 — first overall by the Indianapolis Colts

▶ Father Archie and brother Eli are also NFL quarterbacks.

▶ Led NFL in passer rating three times.

▶ Second all-time behind Brett Favre in passing touchdowns and passing yards.

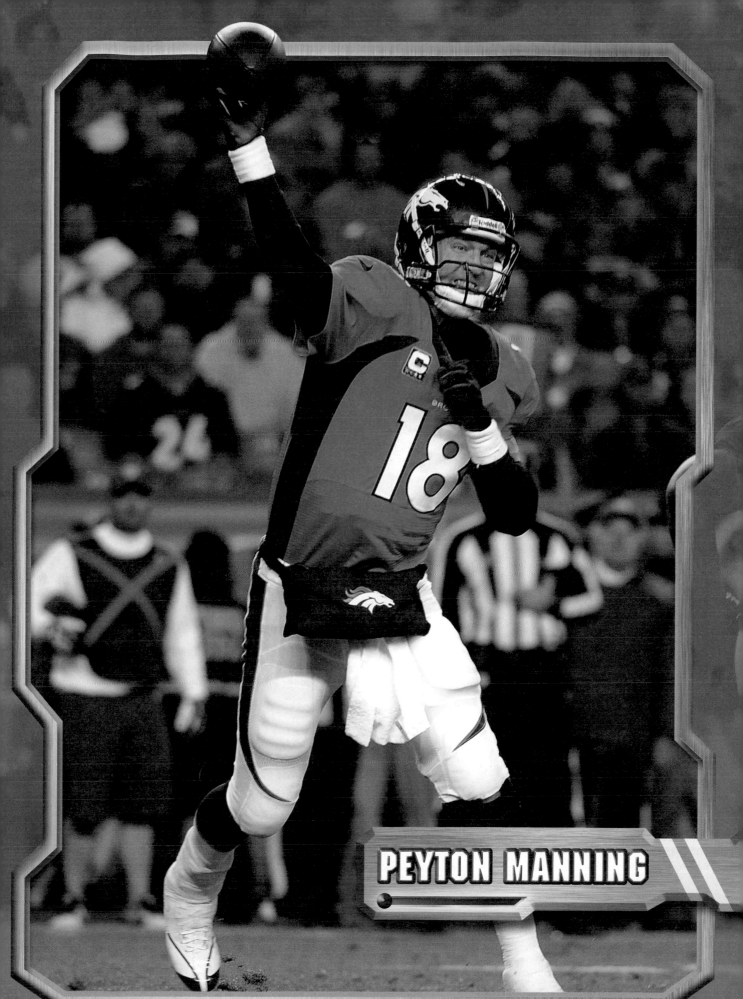

PEYTON MANNING

ROBERT MATHIS

LINEBACKER

There's a saying that you can't teach an old dog new tricks . . . but in the NFL, apparently you can teach an old Colt some pretty good ones. Robert Mathis was one of the NFL's top defensive ends for 10 years. He racked up more than 10 sacks in four different seasons and earned three Pro Bowl trips.

In 2012, however, the Colts made a big move: They switched him from defensive end to linebacker. Mathis's job was still to get at the QB, but now he had to do it from a standing start and sometimes fight through more than one blocker.

No problem.

Mathis proved that his sack-happy ways were just as good from his new position— even better, in fact. In 2013, he set a career high and led the NFL with 19.5 sacks. He forced eight fumbles, also an NFL best.

The 2013 season was the latest in a long line of achievements for Mathis, who grew up in Georgia. He went to a small school, Alabama A&M, and was not drafted until the fifth round. His athletic ability and nose for the quarterback soon earned him a starting spot in Indianapolis. Opposing teams called him a "game-wrecker." He specializes in not only sacking the passer but in stripping the football. One stat site says that more than a third of his 111 career sacks led to a fumble.

Mathis helped the Colts win Super Bowl XLI over Chicago and has earned five Pro Bowl selections. As tough and talented as he is, however, he gives all the credit for his success to his mom, Emma, who worked as a maid while raising her family. "My mom showed me how to be the best I can be," Mathis said.

MATHIS'S BIG DAY

September 29, 2013:
Mathis tied a career high with three sacks as the Denver defense dominated, helping defeat Jacksonville 37–3.

▶ FACT FILE:

Rookie Season	2003
Years in League	11
Sacks	111
Tackles	373
Interceptions	1

ROBERT MATHIS

Height: 6'-2" **Weight:** 235 lbs. **College:** Alabama A&M

* *Drafted in 2003 — fifth round by the Indianapolis Colts*

▶ *Has forced 50 fumbles in NFL career.*

▶ *Scored his only NFL TD on a fumble recovery in 2008.*

▶ *Scored his only career safety in 2013.*

ROBERT MATHIS

LESEAN MCCOY
RUNNING BACK

While NFL passers were making news—and setting records—through the air in 2013, LeSean McCoy was making headlines of his own—on the ground. Thanks to a new offensive game plan, McCoy had his best season as a pro, winning the NFL's rushing title by a wide margin.

McCoy was an outstanding runner at the University of Pittsburgh, breaking several records set by Hall of Famer Tony Dorsett. McCoy took over the starting spot for the Eagles in 2010, his second season in Philadelphia, and never looked back. In 2011, he led the NFL with 17 rushing touchdowns; he was the first Eagles player to do that since the great Steve Van Buren back in 1949. That same year, McCoy had three receiving touchdowns. McCoy is one of the most versatile backs in the league, able to play a big part in the passing game as well as the running game.

And talk about game-breakers—the NFL keeps stats on just about everything, but here's one you probably hadn't known. McCoy has reeled off seven touchdown runs of 40 or more yards in the fourth quarter of games—the most ever.

In 2013, McCoy got some good news. The Eagles got a new coach, Chip Kelly, who is an offensive genius. He made the University of Oregon into a scoring machine. He took over the Eagles and McCoy became the key to the team's return to the top of the NFC East. McCoy led the league with 1,607 rushing yards. That was more than 250 yards ahead of the runner-up.

With more practice in the Kelly system, McCoy and the Eagles expect to make more news in 2014.

McCOY'S BIG DAY

December 8, 2013: All the players in the Eagles game against the Lions were wearing regular cleats, but McCoy looked like he was wearing snowshoes. With snow falling throughout the game and eight inches of the white stuff on the ground, McCoy romped for a team-record 217 yards. A big part of that were touchdown runs of 40 and 57 yards.

▶ FACT FILE:

Rookie Season	2009
Years in League	5
Rushing Attempts	1,149
Rushing Touchdowns	39
Rushing Yards	5,473
Receiving Yards	2,127
Receiving Touchdowns	10

LESEAN MCCOY

Height: 5'-10" Weight: 215 lbs. College: Pittsburgh

*Drafted in 2009 — second round by Philadelphia Eagles

▶ *His 36 total TDs were the most ever for a college player in his first two seasons.*

▶ *Has had at least 40 receptions in every NFL season.*

▶ *Does 100 push-ups right before every game.*

LESEAN MCCOY

Remember Tim Tebow? He can be thanked for injecting a bit of a spark into the NFL a couple of seasons ago. But he can also be thanked, sort of, for helping Cam Newton become one of the top young QBs in the league. When Tebow decided to come back for his senior year at Florida, Newton, his backup, moved from Florida to a junior college and then to Auburn. At Auburn, he found the perfect offense for his powerful running and perfect passing. In his only season there, he blew away the competition. His most famous game came when he led the Tigers back from being 24–0 down to defeat rival Alabama. Newton won the Heisman Trophy and was the No. 1 overall pick of the 2011 season. Thanks, Tim!

With the Panthers, Newton was handed the starting role from the first game . . . and what a first game! Though Carolina lost, he set a rookie passing record and impressed opponents and experts alike. Most thought that such a big player could not succeed as an NFL QB, or that NFL QBs should not run so much. Newton proved them all wrong. By the end of his rookie season, he had set a record for QBs with 14 rushing touchdowns and set a new rookie record with 4,058 passing yards (a mark since topped by Andrew Luck).

In 2013, the Panthers had their best season (yet!) with Newton in charge. They won the NFC South with a 12–4 record. Newton threw 24 TD passes and ran for six more. A disappointing playoff loss means that Newton and the Panthers have something to shoot for in 2014: a Super Bowl spot.

NEWTON'S BIG DAY

September 11, 2011: Talk about a good start: In his first NFL game, Newton set a league rookie record with 422 passing yards. He had two touchdown passes and ran for a third score. (To top himself, he broke his own yardage record a week later.)

▶ FACT FILE:

Rookie Season	2011
Years in League	3
Pass Attempts	1,475
Completions	882
Touchdowns	64
Passing Yards	11,299
Interceptions	42
Career Passer Rating	86.4

CAM NEWTON

Height:	Weight:	College:
6'-5"	260 lbs.	Auburn

* Drafted in 2011 — first overall by the Carolina Panthers

▶ *Ran or threw for a total of 38 touchdowns in his junior college season.*

▶ *Was only the third No. 1 pick to win the national title and a Heisman in the same season.*

▶ *Has four NFL games with two or more rushing touchdowns.*

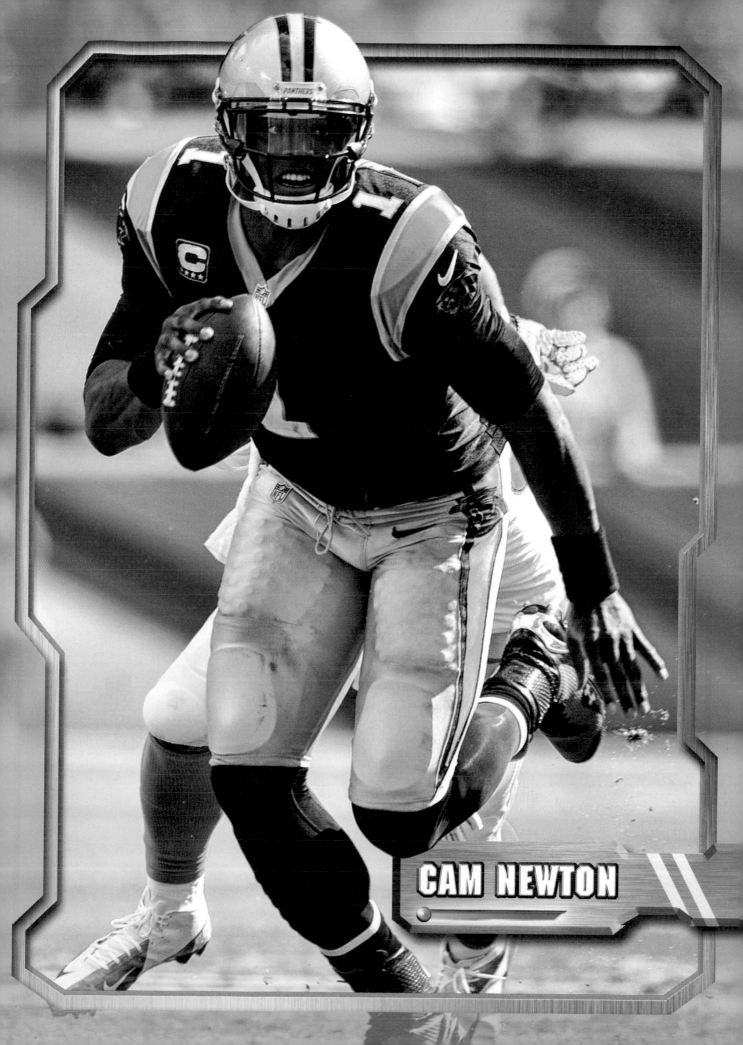

CAM NEWTON

ANDREW LUCK
QUARTERBACK

Most NFL passers first tossed the pigskin around with their dads in the backyard. Andrew Luck did that, but his backyards were in Europe! Luck's dad was also more than just a passing dad—he was a former NFL quarterback. Oliver Luck had moved his family to Germany and then to London while he helped run teams in the NFL's European leagues.

The family returned to America and lived in Houston. Andrew's knowledge of the world made him a great student. That led to a spot at Stanford University in 2009. Stanford is one of the country's top schools, but at the time it was not one of the top football programs. In fact, before Luck took over, the team had not had a winning season in eight years. Luck teamed up with his new coach Jim Harbaugh and turned things around quickly. The young passer combined football smarts with steady nerves and a great arm. He led Stanford to three straight winning seasons and three bowl games.

After his senior season, he won the Maxwell Award as the nation's top player and the Johnny Unitas Golden Arm as the top QB. He also finished second in voting for the Heisman Trophy.

Living up to that amazing record would be a tough job, but Luck was up to the challenge. In 2012, he was taken first overall by the Colts. Indianapolis had let another pretty good quarterback go the year before and needed a replacement. Luck would be filling the shoes of the legendary Peyton Manning.

Just as he had at Stanford, Luck was ready to succeed. In 2011, the Colts had won two games. In 2012, they won 11. Luck also set an NFL rookie record with 4,374 passing yards. To prove it was not a fluke, he did better in 2013, cutting his interceptions in half and improving in completion percentage. And the Colts won 11 more games.

The Colts' QB has traveled a lot of miles to get where he is. And he's showing that it's not Luck . . . it's all skill.

LUCK'S BIG DAY

January 4, 2014: Luck picked a good day to have his best ever: an AFC Wild Card play-off game against Kansas City. He threw for a career-best 443 yards while also passing for four touchdowns. The last one came with about four minutes left and gave the Colts a dramatic 45–44 win.

▶ FACT FILE:

Rookie Season	2012
Years in League	3

▶ *Was the valedictorian (highest-ranked student) in his high school senior class.*

▶ *Named Pac-12 Offensive Player of the Year twice at Stanford.*

▶ *Has made the pro bowl in both of his first two seasons.*

ANDREW LUCK

Height:	Weight:	College:
6'-3"	235 lbs.	Stanford

* *Drafted in 2012, first round by the Indianapolis Colts*

ANDREW LUCK

RICHARD SHERMAN
CORNERBACK

Football games are won with an athlete's hands, feet, body, and heart. You can't win a game by talking about it . . . you have to do it. As it happens, Richard Sherman wins first and talks later. He became a huge story in the NFL in 2013 by helping the Seahawks win big games . . . and then talking up a storm afterward.

Sherman grew up in south Los Angeles. His father was (and still is) a garbage truck driver and his mother worked several jobs. Both parents also worked hard to make sure Sherman studied hard, even as he became a star athlete. His grades and his skills earned him a spot at Stanford University, where he was part of that team's football turnaround. At Stanford, he caught the eye of another college coach, Pete Carroll of USC.

In 2011, Carroll took over the Seahawks and he made Sherman one of his first draft picks. With the rookie as part of a powerful defense, Seattle won 11 games in 2012 and became one of the NFL's elite teams.

Sherman's skill in covering receivers and laying out solid tackles was a key part of the team's success. Sherman also made head-lines by mocking Tom Brady after Seattle defeated the Patriots.

In 2013, Sherman was a key part of a secondary called the Legion of Boom. The Seattle D held teams to a league-low 14.4 points per game. In the NFC Championship Game, Sherman made the key play to send Seattle to the Super Bowl. Right after the game, he was on live TV and spoke about this big play. But it's not bragging if you back it up, as the saying goes. Sherman later helped Seattle whomp Denver in the Super Bowl, 43–8.

Sherman's outgoing personality and football talent (his eight interceptions led the NFL and he made the Pro Bowl) have put him in the spotlight. With a Super Bowl ring on his finger, he's happy to be there.

SHERMAN'S BIG DAY

January 9, 2013: With the game and a Super Bowl spot on the line, Sherman rose high into the air to knock away a game-winning pass. If he hadn't knocked down the ball headed to San Francisco's Michael Crabtree, the Seahawks would not have made it to Super Bowl XLVIII.

▶ FACT FILE:

Rookie Season	2011
Years in League	3
Interceptions	20
Tackles	141

▶ *Sherman was also a top wide receiver in high school.*

▶ *At Stanford, was a Pac-10 All-Freshman team . . . as receiver, before switching to CB as a senior.*

▶ *Has returned two NFL interceptions for touchdowns.*

RICHARD SHERMAN

Height:	Weight:	College:
6'-3"	195 lbs.	Stanford

* Drafted in 2011, fifth round by the Seattle Seahawks

RICHARD SHERMAN

DEZ BRYANT
WIDE RECEIVER

For his first two NFL seasons, Dez Bryant showed flashes of great promise. But he could not put it all together. In his second two seasons, however, he has busted out. After a shaky start, he has become one of the most dangerous pass-catchers in the NFL.

Bryant faced a tough entry to the NFL. An all-state star in the tough Texas high school ranks, he played college ball at Oklahoma State. For two seasons, he was one of the top receivers in the Big 12, as well as a lightning-quick punt returner. As a sophomore, he made an impressive 19 touchdown catches plus had two punt return TDs. But after getting into some trouble off the field he was suspended after only three games in 2009.

In 2010, the Dallas Cowboys took a shot on Bryant's talent, choosing him in the first round. For his first NFL season, he mostly just returned punts (including two for scores). He had some more troubles and some experts worried that he would not be able to truly show off his outstanding athletic skills.

Bryant stuck with it and in 2012, he put it all together. He caught 92 passes for a career-high 1,382 yards and scored 12 times. He was in the NFL's top 10 in all those categories. In 2013, even though every team sent its best cover men against him, he did it again, with 93 more catches and 13 more TDs.

From a bumpy start, Bryant has battled through to reach the top, earning his first Pro Bowl selection after the 2013 season.

BRYANT'S BIG DAY

December 13, 2012: Bryant caught not one but two 58-yard TD passes from Tony Romo. Bryant had 9 total catches for a 224 yards receiving. It was also his seventh straight game with a TD catch, tying a Cowboys record.

► FACT FILE:

Rookie Season	2010
Years in League	4
Receptions	293
Touchdowns	13
Receiving Yards	4,104

DEZ BRYANT

Height:	Weight:	College:
6'-4"	225 lbs.	Oklahoma State

* Drafted in 2010 — first round by the Dallas Cowboys

► He caught 21 touchdown passes as a high school senior.

► Was named to several All-America teams as a sophomore at OSU.

► Against the Ravens in 2012, Bryant had a career-high 13 receptions.

ROOKIES TO WATCH

Who will be the NFL Superstars of the years to come? In 2013, the NFL welcomed a solid group of rookies. Watch for more exciting play from these guys in 2014 and the years ahead.

EDDIE LACY

PACKERS RUNNING BACK

Lacy was the NFL offensive rookie of the year. He ran for 1,178 yards and scored 11 touchdowns. Lacy kept the Packers' playoff hopes alive when star QB Aaron Rodgers missed games due to an injury.

GIOVANI BERNARD

BENGALS RUNNING BACK

A speedy and elusive runner, Bernard had 500 or more yards both rushing and receiving in 2013, scoring eight times. He could play a big role in many parts of the Bengals' offense.

KIKO ALONSO
BILLS LINEBACKER

This hard-hitting linebacker showed he could play both the run and the pass as a rookie. His 159 tackles were third in the NFL and he also intercepted four passes.

TYRANN MATHIEU
CARDINALS DEFENSIVE BACK

The player known as "Honey Badger" was anything but sweet to opponents. In his first NFL season, Mathieu was able to play both cornerback and safety, while also returning punts. His many skills should put him among the top DBs in the league very soon.

KEENAN ALLEN
CHARGERS WIDE RECEIVER

Other than a couple of good early games, Allen started his rookie season slowly. But by the end of it, he and QB Philip Rivers were on the same page. Allen had five TD catches in December as the Chargers won four straight games to earn a playoff berth. Allen ended the season with 71 catches, eight of them for touchdowns.

2013 NFL STANDINGS

AFC EAST
PATRIOTS	12-4
JETS	8-8
DOLPHINS	8-8
BILLS	6-10

AFC NORTH
BENGALS	11-5
STEELERS	8-8
RAVENS	8-8
BROWNS	4-12

AFC SOUTH
COLTS	11-5
TITANS	7-9
JAGUARS	4-12
TEXANS	2-14

AFC WEST
BRONCOS	13-3
CHIEFS	11-5
CHARGERS	9-7
RAIDERS	4-12

NFC EAST
EAGLES	10-6
COWBOYS	8-8
GIANTS	7-9
REDSKINS	3-13

NFC NORTH
PACKERS	8-7-1
BEARS	8-8
LIONS	7-9
VIKINGS	5-10-1

NFC SOUTH
PANTHERS	12-4
SAINTS	11-5
FALCONS	4-12
BUCCANEERS	4-12

NFC WEST
SEAHAWKS	13-3
49ERS	12-4
CARDINALS	10-6
RAMS	7-9

SUPER BOWL XLVIII
SEATTLE SEAHAWKS 43–DENVER BRONCOS 8